BLOOMER

BLOOMER

poems by Jessica Hincapie

Hincapie, Jessica
1st edition

ISBN: 978-1-949487-10-7
Library of Congress Control Number: 2021951024

Interior design by Matt Mauch
Cover art images courtesy of Biodiversity Heritage Library. http://www.bioiverstiylibrary.org
Cover design by Tori Baisden
Editing by Matt Mauch and Halee Kirkword
Assistant editing by Hadley Hendrix

Trio House Press, Inc.
Ponte Vedra Beach, FL

To contact the author, send an email to tayveneese@gmail.com.

For Catherine and Oscar
and for home

TABLE OF CONTENTS

/

//

Joy has been a habit. Suddenly this rain.

– Jack Gilbert

Yes, I deserve a spring—I owe nobody nothing.

– Virginia Woolf

Coping Mechanism

All around town, the bricklayers bury the roses.
The railroad kids graffiti the train cars
making them look like ancient metal elephants
linked trunk to tail, on and on. The kids rattle
cans of paint, yet their heart-sounds are louder.
Who knew being in love this long would reveal
that I am not kind by nature like I was raised
to believe. Unable to make those around me
happy through sheer will only. Mary Shelley
kept a lock of her husband's hair
and a piece of his formaldehyded heart
wrapped in one of his poems. Would cry
at night over the black bounty, but sometimes
salt shrinks the heart the same way it would a snail.
Crying is as useful as a sock of soap.
Which party gets to sigh in relief after the beating?
Even now, the sound of plates
being thrown against the wall of our garage. A new
coping mechanism the therapist recommended.
Of all the opposites I've been holding,
this one is heaviest. That around the corner from us,
there is always a street parade ending
or a garlic factory on fire. The smell amazing,
but the damage expansive and irreversible.
Of my own coping? It's negotiable.
Depends on which serial killers have just been I.D.'d
after years quiet in Wyoming. Depends on
how cool the air is after a good rain.
I would pull out my own heart, shave off
small slivers for keepsakes if it could guarantee you
remembering me. Surely this is how you bury
the stars that won't clash fast enough to make planets.
Surely this is how you observe the darkness
without trying to set it on fire.

The Breakup of My Country

I lived through the breakup of my country,
content to catch the leaking ceiling water
with my own mouth. Mother wanted
more for me, wanted me queen
of the shiny mountains of silverware and various
neighborhood roundabouts.
It had just come out in the news
that the Monopoly man had made his fortune
off slanging candy to the railroad kids
and everyone had an opinion.
Those days were a string of emotional
and geological terrors. 1960's spacemen
in their one-dollar convertibles, and twenty-four-hour
sobriety chips tossed into the trash.
Everyone wanted to start believing in things
with their eyes closed.
For once, the truth felt like a thrill.
There was a week we were all sweating on Monday
but by Wednesday it was snowing,
the strange weather conjuring repressed memories
too vivid to be accurate.
Like the hurricane that rolled in one year,
suddenly and all at once. How father left
us waiting in a closet during the eye,
while he used those two quiet minutes
for throwing the loose patio furniture
to the bottom of the swimming pool.
What wasn't submerged in the morning
was assumed gone forever, and
everything that happened after that
felt like it was happening to me.

Postlapsarian Poem

Lets not talk of Oblivion
or who might be at that party.

There were whole groups of people
whose sole jobs were to pray

for the King's absolution. Day in
and out with rosaries around the wrists.

And what of their own sins? Who prayed
for them when they kicked the dog,

overwatered the Hydrangeas?
Who prays for me, now that I've

stopped praying for others? Surely not
my atheist lover or the man who butchers

my meats and knows there is no
bleeding sheep nailed to my front door.

I have come to accept that we don't
know all things. Or is it that

we don't all know things.
The distinction is important.

As long as I'm not the only one
in the dark, I can live there happily

making out shapes by squinting,
hollering at every opossum loitering

on the fence posts. It's that there might
be those out there who are further along

that I can't seem to stand. Envious of the noises
they make, the small lifeguard whistles

they were given at birth by some ghost
hiding behind the curtain during the baptism.

Of course it is not their fault that we should live
this life cloistered, wandering to pass the time.

That we can't conceive of the tablecloth being ripped
away without the disturbance of a single glass.

That we might misunderstand the lullaby for an end.

On the One Hand [In the Other]

It seems that the people in my life have become too real
to write about, making poetry a suitable space only for strangers.

The woman at the cemetery, missed by seconds. Her lipstick
kisses still fresh on the marble grave next to Papito's.

There was the girl met in group therapy, whose dealer,
named Temple, blesses every batch of mushrooms he sells.

These days, my houseguests are always at odds with my house
ghosts. The stairwell constantly littered with tin cans

and lynched cats. Obvious death threats, but from
the guests or the ghosts, I have yet to determine.

I've folded these phantoms into talismans time and time again.
Still, each year presents itself like a small tight coin.

A fountain of fish I've mistaken for silver. This life
will ask you more than once to make the choice

between starfish or worm. One animal growing back
what was lost, the other learning to live without.

Micromanaging

Have you ever watched someone disappear
into a suitcase? It begins with one leg at a time,

arms folded around the torso. You must zip
it closed with your own teeth. There was once

this contortionist – tiny like my grandmother.
Instead of the suitcase, she folded herself

into a paper crane

before sealing herself inside a mason jar
she brought from her own kitchen.

"Paprika" still stuck to the front.
We met backstage where I asked her how

she made herself so small. She said to imagine
a pizza with one slice missing. Was she talking

about the whole pie or the missing slice?
She said 'Neither, it's about being

the goddamn cheese.'

Finally, some sense of space. My body bending
towards corners, towards the empty side of

the His and Her closets I'd find in my friends'
houses. Angling itself anywhere the light can't reach.

Baby steps. Don't you see?

Soon I will be small enough to fit
inside the suitcase. Soon I will dismantle myself

completely, ascend into air and join all the tender
dust that settles on ceiling fans and desk lamps.

When I Was Sixteen

I cut off my black hair,
sold it to save a life. My brother
was still eating tender meats, my father
disappearing every now and then
into the sandy dunes.

A boy I liked played in a Christian
rock band. Smoking joints behind
the neon cross of the Mega Church
we could hear the congregation wailing
a mile past the tree line.

Amen Dancing
he called it, mimicking limbs
like flurries of ice, eyes rolled toward
the sky in supplication.

When I was sixteen I pierced
too many places and drew the bath
right up to the lip of the tub.

Believed in God more
but felt God's presence less.

Days when I was happy,
poetry seemed useless.
But then that thought made me sad, and so
I remembered poetry.

Remembered the halogens
in the public lakes that made the kids
glow phosphorescent
under lamplight.

When I was sixteen I discovered
the jar of sorrows and plagues sitting
patiently by the glittering pool of my patio.

What else was I to do
but open it?

Shake each creature's hand and clap
as they cannonballed
into the deep end—unbothered
by where they went after that.

At the end of that summer
the city Swap Shop set up a drive-in theater.
Projected movies right against
its cracking yellow façade.

We would hide boys under blankets
in the beds of our trucks and get away
with two tickets only.

It was a wishful time of spoiled
fruit and red elbows, trying to learn better
ways of eating living things.
Friends spitting seeds from the tops
of condos down into the event horizon.

Sometimes when we kept quiet long enough,
we could hear those glossolalists
and their Amen Dancing
lifting up, out of that church, spreading
over the swamps and suburbs.

How the voices stayed like that
the entire night, suspended
like angels in their makeshift sonnets,

fragmenting the night's reality
into small fists of light and sound.

The Dead and I Sing Behind the Rhododendron Bushes

I am older now and better at loving. At least that's what I wanted
to write on the "Where Are They Now" section of my high school
reunion pamphlet. Instead I say something like,
these days I cry and he gets hard. These days no one corrects

the idle beachcombers collecting sand dollars,
not realizing they are the skeletons of sea urchins. What little green you see,
their last bit of life. I don't say any of this. I don't mention my job,
but instead mention the many hours in traffic spent daydreaming of careening

into the intersection, because collision can also be a form
of communion. I wanted them to see that they too could make lights
flicker just by looking. That this bloodletting would not follow us
into our dreams. And I am not the first person

to go missing like this. Fighting back the Floridian in me for miles. Each
return like an immense cloud of mayflies I keep having to walk through.
Forever, a dog chained to a fence, a politician found in a motel bed.
Boys catching snakes with bare hands and brown paper bags.

What they don't tell you is that living below sea level for so long leaves
behind a thirst nowhere else can quench. Not when you've seen for sure,
waters just deep enough to walk through them fully submerged.
A whole human length of blue. Those kinds of things always leave you

bargaining. Like the summer I broke my ankle, and my friend kept
pinching me hard, saying that the body couldn't hold two pains at one time
and it would choose for me. That if she pinched me enough maybe it would
pick that pain instead. I was better at loving back then,

or at least better at believing in love. When believing didn't require
currency or allegiance. Wouldn't take from you past what you had to offer.
After they removed the soft-cast from my leg, we spent the rest of that
summer riding our bikes around town, stopping to lay in wet grassy fields.

Once catching glimpse of a rancher's daughter branding her horses
at dusk. How the next morning we returned to watch the horses curtsy
before letting her mount. Knowing that the worst thing
she could ever do to them, she had already done.

Stand-In for a Ghost at a Séance

Brianna's father leaves Tupperware filled with water
behind every doorjamb when practicing his Santeria.

For months a stagnant palm-sized pond sits in her
bedroom. Mosquitos swarm, sweating themselves dry.

Gorging once more on water laced with bloodhoney
and vinegar. After the accidents she says he can heal

my awful luck with three Virgin candles and a live chicken.
I am two clenched fists the entire time, the same shape

I took at birth, I know what I have in my hands.
Now, during every family reunion Brianna and I

make like lambs and slit our throats on stage. Since we
were girls we've known what sacrifices a party like this

needs to continue. I have a body for a few reasons.
And that's always one way of looking at it.

Winner

Eventually I will witness a perfect crime and
not recognize it as my very own life.
I leave the house and smell barbeque,
find out later it was forest fire.
The TV keeps telling me to freeze my eggs
but not my anxieties, so I am uninterested.
These days the poems are more like
scions of misunderstandings. You said ————
I heard ———— . And it spins off from there.
My next move calling out to me in a game of telephone.
Whether or not to listen, to gather out on the cliffs
with my swarm of swine, wearing the hurried curls
of my grandmother. There's the rub.
You must be born with a taste for this kind of life.
Picking baby names off tombstones, laughing
only to bring on hysteria. Ordering cured meats,
grateful for the knowledge received
from eating something older than myself.
I doubt I will grow out of fancies such as these.
Out of my liminal self, the one who
panthers into the party wearing only satin panties,
telling everyone about the time I read in a big book
that women bruise easier than men because
unlike crates of peaches in the back of a truck
women are peaches in pudding in the back of a truck,
or something scientific like that.

Trash Fish

It's happening all throughout the city—
people losing money, hearts breaking in bedrooms
above bars, and more murders
along the scenic routes than the radio would like to admit.

We try escaping to the lake to swim and drink
margarita goo from juice pouches. Feeling
lawless and untangled when near bodies of water.
No one bringing up Grandpa's wandering hand,
Brother with his hospital rooms, Father with love
always shifting into second gear.

We assume there will be time for that later,
during the reading of wills and palms, and anyway
the real secret of the weekend is that I am afraid
of what is growing inside of me. A tumor
or a child not yet a child, more like a leaf.

How easy it could be to crush it under my foot.
Keep it secret forever until it went dark, because
all secrets turn dark. Isn't that the truth of family?

The whole weekend blue carp crowd the waters.
By the docks, eating barnacles off the bottom
of boats. On the shore, washed up and warm. Bellies
blue and silver in the sand.

The locals are unmoved by the trash fish,
even at dinner, when we wait dockside
next to a man-made hole where patrons can pay
a quarter for feeding the fish dog food.

The night zeros in on a young boy teetering
around the hole, throwing pellets at the carp
like a lowercase hades. The fish are hungry for food,
and the boy hungry for control when suddenly

he slips into the water. The carps' crazed thrashing
too much for anyone to stare straight at.
Dinner ruined for everyone and the night carrying on
with its small promises of loss. Sweat that tastes of rain.

Bizzaro World

For Brian

Opposition everywhere. That is
the truth of love. Like wolves
coming across a field full of lambs,
vision goes totally grotesque
near the flock. A few hearts
get galvanized by the sight
of such tumult. But it doesn't stop us.
In the mirror we make funny faces, press
hands against glass for entrance
into the other world.
One in which you always
tender in extremes.
Casting pearls into bog water,
cuffs folded from the ankles.
Was it ever going to get easier?
This skin of us
like the warmth of clay in a kiln,
toughening into something breakable
and sure of its strength all at once.
And that is to say punctured but
still breathing. That is to say
unsure of everything else.

Freeze Warning

Frost on the swamp, the mangrove's many legs folding in from the freeze.
You were away again, for once thinking of me. I was sure of it.
Winter should not have been that cold, but I was becoming something new
and so did not mind. Such imperceptible shifts;
when reaching for a hanger in the closet
the feeling of a hand surely reaching back between the blouses.
Meanwhile at night, I could hear in my dreaming the sound
of your boots in high grass, scattering
the cactus aphids away with your loom.
The Mylar birds got tied up in the telephone wires that year
sending crossed signals out over town
in the shape of extra-celestial ships.
And the oysters, which the men at the marina swear
taste just like the seas they're pulled from (so that the difference
is obvious whether Bahamian Waters, Pure Atlantic, or Gulf),
even they were not cooperating. Mysteriously salt-less after shucking.
Love from that angle looked much like missing you.
But a new world was being built in the image of someone having just left
the room—empty diner booth, echo of exit bell,
change still on the table from a generous tip.
In the desert you laugh and the honking sends all the bicuspids
into the sand. Strange how it is only now that I can see you clearly.
How long you must have waited in the grass
for a perfect moment to wrangle the rattlesnake with your pin-hook,
pluck out its fangs. A gift, which still sits in a small glass jar by the bed.
Is there an odyssey more perilous than young love, dumb to its core?
Hot and petulant as thrush on a baby's tongue. That winter was loaded
with symbols and not one worth reading correctly.
The feeling of a car moving forward despite being in park.
Sand in back molars, stars sharp as caltrops.
Everything acting out like a hungry kid.

Of The Final Spring

The poets will have this to say: (   ).
And perhaps the birds will echo it
as sure as the light which slits
through trees, as sure as the alchemical
frogs we gave up on years ago.
Earth was deep and glowing and filled
with babies. Carrying them all
over her own body, the way a mother
spider would. Oh drop. Oh initial,
sudden brood.

There'd been a brief moment
when I thought we'd be happy, wanted terribly
to close the gap.
But all of the candy was being made
with soft chewy centers and soon the same
would be said of people. The whole lot of us wanting
to do away with the disco
totem, the myth about the flood.

Some days this whole house of me creaks,
and I wish I could lift up the skirt
of my own anxiety and clown cry
at the outrageous husk.
Gel in hair, small flashing lights
in the soles of sneakers. Constantly shoving
my jabber behind the couch cushions
at friends' parties or leaving my rise
in the ladies room.

When will it again be appropriate to return
to the heart in the jar, to the glitter
in the gutter from the street parade,
making the sewer rats sparkle?

This room I've built to hold
what ought to be true
is collapsing fast as skin.

But even now there's still the chance
I might be given a new name,
one in length with grace.
A chance to be new to everyone before.
To everyone who finds me after.

Fishbowl Living

What separates me from my life
is a see-through thing.
Jellyfish membrane,
fragrant flower sealed
in wax, its smell kept secret.

Always the plastic
shower curtain with a lover
naked on the other side,
memories that exist
only through photos.

There are holes in the soft ground
where the mudskippers
find new exits. There are days
when I do not question
my friends when they talk
about their depression.

Is there a better way? Will I
learn it in time? The night
shares with me its necessary
illusions, and I share
with it mine in return.

The rookery of glass pigeons,
the portmanteaus
of skinned light. Which was
the first painting of a painting?
Can a soul be like that?

Bloomer

The entire world had cut to the scene
in which the widow buries her dead lover's bones.

We'd been close to summer for over two weeks.
Every walk, I saw a gallow in the skyline.
You went to grab my hand.

Less anxious,
if I were less anxious maybe.

I've never before lived around these many flowers:

the phlox
        and bee balm,
                the watermelon cone blossoms.

Under the midday sun they shrink back,
but when I wake early enough, after the morning's heat
has met night's air to make dew,
I can see them in full, petals stretching east.

It made sense at the time that we would call forth
something of a different world and wait patiently
for it to answer our questions.

About the moonlight.
About the slow response of lovers and
God's timed expression of death.

It all seemed in sequence with our faith, despite
being a time with not one single satisfied pew in church.
A time where not one whale made it safely
back in the water once it was out.

Of course the comrades and I believed we could do it.
Turn a stone into a bird without anyone noticing
—or maybe with everyone noticing.

But we were late bloomers, lazy hearts.
It was easy to want life to be good for everyone.
Harder to understand why it was not.

Munda Arriba

after Mamita

Yes, you look around and it's all bad.
Always been all bad. Randy Johnson
explodes a bird with one pitch.
A tree catches fire from the inside.
The paper says Amelia Earhart's
bones have been identified:
Cause of death unclear, most likely
Sand Crabs. You walk
out of your house slower this morning,
afraid to trip the invisible wire.
But every mean thing, every first swing
at someone's shadow, it's all
on its way to meet you at the door.
Should you have listened when you
were told to find a man who still believes
in war? Should you have kept
it all closer to the chest, your voice
lower when it asked for love?
Made better choices? The times you laid out
in the field, unconscious of what breathed
between the blades. Careful child,
we could be here all day. History continues
stringing along its inimical cabbages.
You came out crying and haven't
stopped since.

Inheritance

As girls of the cul-de-sac it was our job to show the new ones
how it was done. Show them the head full of bees, the shapes
we continued to resurrect before getting it right.
Little Lavinias with our hair on fire, good luck before war—
or tongues torn out for theatrics. Silence the new opposite of tragedy.

We'd stand in a straight line, shoulder deep in chlorine, legs open
below the water to form a tunnel for the new girls to swim through.
We'd wait until they'd get right to the middle,
then on the count of one, two

we'd close our legs to trap them. Laugh as they tried to find
their way to the surface. We all took turns
swimming through the tunnel, convinced we were the ones
fast enough to make it through to the other side.
It continued this way, in and out of the water.

And maybe it all comes down to narrative.
To the name you give a thing before you know it intimately.
So of course they said we taught the game to ourselves.

Even though the man bit my mother during a work function
and Pastor made all us girls promise: wed, bed, *then* bled
(Did I say bled? I meant blessed). Even when the boys we met
demanded love, wanted blood on the downy pillows as proof,

while their mothers clipped coupons and would not shake our hands.
When the muggers of both my grandmothers
closed the space between hand and swath of neck.

We'd been coming along nicely before that. Now we let
the flowers wilt on purpose, death not always unbecoming.
We wonder what pretty horses there must be in places
where horses run wild. We keep the new girls underwater
for longer and longer. Each gasping breath a new bright start.

Seconds Before the Squall

And all that's left outside are the horses
tied to their posts. When the floods
recede will we line up the dead
in neat rows, the way we did
in Ypres? The last children
are leaving their homes now.
Soon only loose fur, aglets without
laces, shores of nothing more
than the dismantled spines
of jellyfish. Riddance swelling
among the barren fruit flies, their
kingdom of peels and pits.
The girls swat, no use. Pierce
their tongues instead. Their fathers
well toward retiring now, *if only*
those jack asses in office.
Today the ability to hunt boar
by hot air balloon was made legal.
It should then reason that we too
were once abused animals
scratching at doors while
water rose over us. Have
all hid from the rainbow
giant in the sky who wants us
dead by rifle. Who's to say
any one of us hasn't already died,
isn't right now covered
by white linens? Thoroughbreds
with all their weight piled
atop their own limbs
leaving cracks in the metal soles. It is natural
for disasters to beget more disaster.
If you haven't already, set fire
to something while it's raining.
The juxtaposition will feel
like an orgasm, not sure
when you inhale if you are
breathing in smoke or steam.

Bury Me

Bury me in anything made of wood.
Even if it takes decades, I want there to be a way out.
Whatever you do, no matter what the caretaker says,
please don't bury me wearing a bra. Not even if
all the other dead women are doing it.
Don't flatten my curls. I won't need anything beautiful,
just the jealous wingspan of God's eyelash.
When I was born the women in the town all fell
under fever spells, despite the snow already forming
on the fields, the buff and speckled ducks hiding out
in the priory's stables. It seems pure that even in the afterlife
this dark heritage would follow. That certain myths heard
in childhood would be confirmed true.
The one that says Courtney Love auditioned
for The Mickey Mouse Club with a Plath poem about incest.
The Chupacabra who ripped its way through
my Great Great Grandfather's farm
draining the blood from the bodies of cows.
Other than these, I will have nothing to show for myself
when Peter, with his necklace of fresh fish,
asks me how I lived. And even if I lie would he still see
how sometimes I wanted badly to bully
anyone who would let me. Or that I was never able
to love those who didn't love me back.
Will he know that I enjoyed the bruising?
That despite the bruises I bought dresses,
like maybe someone would think of me on my knees.
The kind of person who likes wearing the wound.
And when he asks of what I saw,
will I tell him of the sinkholes and swamps?
The complications of my father's pocket watch?
Or will I settle on the plastic flamingos
that outnumbered the real flamingos ten to one?
How swift he will pull back the rope.
How mischievous the final miracle.
I can hear them all laughing, even now, in a nice way,
at my many misunderstandings. Can see the doors
I should have walked through, each greeting me
the way animals who return home
greet one another for returning.

Play For Keeps

It has become harder and harder to collect the days.
Water drips from the faucets into the plastic bins,
saved for boiling. A small jewel of poisoned juice
on the kitchen sill for the ants to take back
to the queen, only true method of eradication.
I am missing the slow burn of autumn.
Everything now is too lush. The screen door
a constant buzz, brimming with life so small I could squash it
if only I could see it. In vain, I try to gather all of the unaccounted
hours of summer, squeeze them into the space between the white linens
billowing and the French doors, in hopes
we might sleep easier. Might set fire to the ledger
we are keeping of each other's half-truths. What tempest
took us this far out to sea? Sailors gathering under the small
respite of rain, to gamble their tokens away under dim moon.
To have a soul that resembles more a small stone
worried over by greasy thumbs. I want to believe
in you, Universe. In our mutually vested interest in the script.
But I keep having to tell strangers I meet that it takes less energy
to believe in magic than to convince yourself of coincidence.
And I must say it with gusto. Even on days I am not certain.

It Shouldn't Take Long to Notice Something is Off

The fauna has turned frantic this season. A record year for rainfall
having made a jungle of the inland areas. Despite this, there are still
tangles of tourists traipsing the sands. Still a mess of Spring Breakers
the year-rounders will synonymize with plastics and balcony death
—a local truth, harsh like they are.

At the party, the girl in glow-gear kept showing us her tattoo
of a Waffle House hoisted high on its chicken feet. *The ghouls
will get us if we don't know where to look and the trickiest women are great
at hiding plainly.* The kitchen bulbs had been replaced with strobes,
& 'Keats and Yeats are On Your Side' was playing in the background.
We should've known this soft doom would follow us home.

That these nights afloat the unlit highways are all diseased. Careening
into the feeder, the only God keeping our car from running off-road
comes in the form of a break light from the car in front. Briefly lighting
the highway lines. How long have we been driving behind somebody?

I've never considered myself a reckless person, but
there is an air of obscenity to even the most harmless of life.
And we can keep swearing up and down we didn't strap ourselves in.
Didn't willingly give our lives to the unhinged Ferris wheel

rolling out into the sea. Brilliant ignorance, like in every noir thriller
where there is always a boardwalk and a body gone. Not dead,
maybe just missing. And you can sense danger
but you aren't sure of it, because nights like these will trick you
into thinking that the disappearing can be beautiful too.

While Everyone Tries to Re-Mystify Life with Art

In Austin, my lover leaves another pair of jeans
in the freezer for the feel of raw denim and I am suckled
by strange dreams for days. Acrobats
in Tangiers performing seven stories tall,
how the boy climbs over the other boy's body.
Or most recently, of a room in midland Texas
where a woman parts her legs and the person watching
thinks only of the hidden muscle holding her
and the world together. I do not write a word for weeks
and pray that this constant wanting of more must mean I am alive.
There are really only two questions
that ever need answering. What do you love
and when will you lose it? I am exhausted of being hungry
all of the time but I cannot forget the canopy
of mango trees, and the small mound
of sand for the flagpole to push through.
Menagerie of still, a day with no excess.
The earth feeling filled to its brim. Oranges for every ferry ride
and daisies, so many puny daisies.
I still believe the answer will come to me without my
even having to call it by name.
I've caught gentler things in my hands before.
But even now, I am yearning for what I can't keep
count of. The irises blooming in the thick polemic summer,
the running of honey from the spoon. I suppose
I must be patient with the other, less obvious things.
Must cease with wringing the neck
of every white bird that comes my way.

Crawfish Season

No foreplay
like watching a lover's
fingers meticulously
peel away at crawfish parts.
Squeeze and slurp out
the heads and various insides
like a vampire playing host
at a Christmas party.
People pay good money
to be front row at the mukbang.
Seductively eyeing
the cornhusks
as if mercy is a thing
that comes cored.
Yes, from time to time
it's the ultimate place-putter,
seeing first hand
how we'll crack a thing open
to get to the life of it.

Nothing Sans Dark

True, it's always difficult to have a body. But think of all
the nice things we can wear. That yeast can develop
in the mouth is no reason to stop inching ourselves
away from death. Toward fancy tailored suits. Mints
on the pillow. No need to be anything but the comedian
at the fashion show. If you can't say anything nice, say
I'm not convinced you exist. But there's a lovely
fragrance in the air. Who cares you can't give blood
because of mad cow. How about a real world
example of pain that doesn't belong to you? How about
the depth of a lake unmoved by the presence of stones?
Ample evidence suggests that nothing sans dark can do
good. Gandhi would sleep naked side by side his niece.
A test of temptation. He never was,   tempted.
You wonder about the girl. Was she able to sleep
any of those nights? All bruises happen without you
noticing. If your spouse kills you do the caretakers
know better than to bury you in your wedding ring?
This doesn't apply to your bruises specifically
but you feel it should be asked. How else to sound
the angels, how else to prepare fear for a feast,
chiffon on every guest, iced over every cake?
More than once, your throat has become a funhouse
tunnel where the ground stays still but the walls spin
and spin. This too will pass. You keep wondering about the girl.
Never mind the girl. She doesn't belong to you either.
Back in the body, they are cleaning the church bells.

Catch a Tiger

When I was young I always had a hard time choosing for fear of choosing
wrong. Uncomfortable shaking even the smallest leaf. Were there moments?
Sure. A fist mid-flight, a perfectly timed pirouette. The day those teens tied
the python to their truck, driving out of the Everglades onto the I-95.
How I went home and touched myself to see if something inside touched back.

They say the most dangerous time in a man's life is when he no longer
understands what he is. For a woman the most dangerous time
must be when she finally does. Perhaps that's why I like it when he
chokes me, because then I don't have to choose. In the kitchen, a kettle
sweats its whistle and he is always close by to bring it off. Minutes later

the smell of fat, and him in the middle of pinching salt into a pot.
It is like this all summer until the green gets to me and August begs us to strip
the bed of its sheets and pin them to the line in the yard. When we were girls,
we believed we'd invented a game to help us choose. And only once
the outcome had been set would we realize what we truly wanted.

Coming of Age

He brings home flowers but we have no vase.
Now the lily's blooming in a beer stein.
I desperately want to feel grown, but there is no
undisclosed spell, no glory in trading
one curb-couch for another and calling it progress.
In Scandinavia young girls castrate deer with their teeth
to turn into Women. We snag twenties
from Dad's cash clip when the house is tight inside.
At twelve we read a book about coming of age rituals,
lingering over pictures of the girl from Bali with red beads
in her hair. How she opened her mouth wide enough
for her canine teeth to be filed down, with them
the sharp edge of sin dulling. *Just like this*,
I was sure the world would one day say,
showing me its secret stones. Truth without its baby teeth.
We got close once without even knowing it.
That night around the bonfire, when the girl in the circle
shared she'd had her first kiss with a boy
who in two years would take a hammer to both
his parents' heads, then throw a house party for his friends.
The bodies locked off in the master bedroom.
How close a first and a last thing touch,
how final every new start. But that's how these things
tend to go. The future always happens anyway.
I remember she said he tasted like licorice.

What We Build

After Sarah Winchester and what she built.

DOOR

The famous poet says
our generation is obsessed with violence.

In the bedroom, in the body.
Anywhere the gun can go off.

And yes, it is true
humans have complicated every gift.

But each hole in this earth
alludes to a center.

SUNROOM

In 1866, The Winchester Arms Company builds
its first repeating rifle.

A gun to win the west.

Soon after, William Winchester, the sole
heir to the dynasty dies.

His wife Sarah inherits the infamous fortune.

DOOR

In one version of the story,
widowed Sarah consults a spiritualist,
after seeing a figure in the shape
of her dead father waving a Yellowboy
rifle at her from across the lake.

She is told to move West
to California to begin construction
on her unending mansion.

Alive as long
as the hammer pounds.

PARLOR

Entering into the house is to stand
in the center of a still birth.
Untouched organ pump. Cross-stitched

pillows puffy from misuse.
The only light in the room channeled
through a single Tiffany Oxeye.

As a girl, they called her Sallie
Belle of New Haven. But
she was more interested in

books about Masonic mazes,
lines from Lewis Carroll poems.

Her interests sat squarely
on the master blueprint of the world.
Imagination her one weapon
in her war with reality.

The house would be
in tribute to these wonders.

Rooms within rooms,
her house is a mimicry of this
portmanteau planet,
cubist dimension of heaven.

Secret messages of Shakespeare
in mosaic. Pythagorean postulates
carved into crown molding.

Small doors opening into large rooms.
Large doors opening into mouse
houses with painted pocket furniture.

A forced perspective.

In this version of the story
she is a genius moving us through

her Rubik's Cube way of understanding
both the number and the leaf,
the matrix for this meanwhile.

HALLWAY

I thought I'd be better at this by now.
Better at smiling through the junk mail,
at believing in heaven for the both of us.

How badly I pray we are not just a miraculous
conjunction of our worst moments.
Our lost in the woods, locked in the bedroom,

bottom of the bottle moments. The silver
stolen, the things you shouldn't have smoked.
The love you strangled or scratched out.

But who isn't drawn straight into darkness,
into the aching holes of tree trunks, the kind
that can fit whole bodies?

Towards the hard things with soft bellies,
like turtles or the mothers of serial killers,
their hands like knotty pine, constantly wringing.

Perhaps this is what draws me to Sarah.
Not her pain, but what she was able
to build with that pain. What she wasn't
willing to destroy with it.

DOOR

Even though I haven't lived at home in almost ten years,
my mother calls me after the shooting to see if I am safe.

Another high school, an old rival one, where I'd sit in the bleachers
as a girl, yelling louder to make up for not having home court advantage.

During my senior year, I'd finally made it to third base.
I'd decided to be a writer. I'd never seen a dead body.

I try not to think about it. Months later I will call my mother
after a different shooting to see if she is safe.

Will our children inherit this earth or just its theaters of war?

VESTIBULE

Kahn says the architect's job is to make space
thoughtful. Pressed seashell in wet cement.
Color of French Revolution in the patina.

In the space between Sarah and I
there is an illegible self that is equal parts woman,
equal parts dark room with a single window.

I believe this is how the Architect survives.
She has not forgotten the moon outside that window.
She has not stopped praying for more thoughtful spaces.

BALLROOM

Not one nail

> you would have heard
> her brag to the guests.

> > *Just like Solomon's Temple*
> > *not one single nail*
> > *holding the whole room up.*

You would have heard her

> brag to the guests if only she'd been
> inclined to invite any.

> > Sarah believed her intelligence
> > was what made her lonely.
> > She could quote Shakespeare,

and Baudelaire. *Her brain,*

> *proved female of the soul.*
> She made visible the insides

> > of the labyrinth.
> > Took pains to braid
> > the unsayable into one plait.

The ballroom is most known

> for how empty it remained
> throughout her life.

> > Appearing as Grand Central
> > might in a dream, vast and void
> > of all travelers.

The only sound to bounce

      against the parquet floors
      was an iron bell in a small ceiling crest

         she used to signal
         the séance hours.

SKYLIGHT

Sarah rings the iron bell once at twelve,
      again at two. Moves from room to room
sleeping in a different bed each night just to confuse
      what lives in the walls. I'd like
to have conviction in anything beyond death,
      but there is little biology can't prove.
If I am made of cells, I hope they are less scientific
      and more akin to the cells of a monastery.
One in which my anchorite daughters roost
      amongst the monks and their religious texts.
Until one day the youngest submerges herself
      into the nearby river. Using the weight
of water to replicate the sensation of touch,
      already aware that in life's final myth
the body too will walk away from you.

MIRROR

What the heart does.
What the heart does is frightening.

Things get doubled in glass,
in shadow, in water, in eyes.

Today the tour guides will tell you
it was clean madness.

A reclusive widow in the throes
of grief and guilt, nervous

about her inheritance tied
to the trigger. Turned crazy

because of the bullet-holed
bodies drying out in the mud.

A forced perspective.

Meanwhile, the only safe
in the house holds no money.

Just a picture of the late Mr. Winchester
and a lock of their dead infant's hair.

DOOR

Out of the 100 plus doors in the manor
few actually lead anywhere.
Most open up to brick walls or drop off
into roomlessness—staircases ascending
into sky. Sarah's private joke.

PICTURE WINDOW

In a different version of the story, Sarah believes she is the reincarnation of
Francis Bacon. In this version she believes Francis Bacon is the true author
of Shakespeare's works. By proxy, in this version, she must also believe she is
Shakespeare.

I am delighted by this version. In thinking of her house as a masterpiece as
precious as Hamlet or Alligator. And why not? All is subject to association.
After the 1906 San Jose Earthquake, Sarah refuses to rebuild what's broken.
She is fond of the ruins, of the naked thought. Ghosts of a different sort.

Sarah knows something we don't. That is what her house tells us.
Like the tiny mantis shrimp which lives in the darkest ocean and has tens
of octal receptors. How it sees past color into time and space itself,
can even see the overlay of lives lived, as if they were living presently.

Palimpsest for this dogged earth, Sarah understood that the strands
were woven, the days like beads of ice on branches of a very large tree.
In this version she is what the mathematicians would call
the immaterial middle point of arc.

BEDROOM

For five full nights there were police stationed
outside the park by our house. Not because
of any crime in particular, but more because of
crimes anticipated. And while I know nothing
will come of it, I still find myself digressing toward
other odd angles. The windows in the house
that may have screens torn, dowels undone
by the sliding doors. The way my friend says
she feels followed by her past, and I immediately
imagine a man. Send her pepper spray to loop
through her purse. And perhaps I've sentenced
us both without even meaning to. My lover
wanting to hamper down the mania in his life,
not yet figuring out that the mania is me.
A stench, clean and fistful. Haven't we all
thought through the darkest of scenarios
and pictured the worst we could do?

DOOR

It is 1895. Teddy Roosevelt brings
down a white male rhino during
his famed African safari.

Photo'd with his favorite
Winchester rifle.

DOOR

*Don't know how to shoot well,
but know how to shoot often.*

DOOR

A point of axis among men.

DOOR

This year, for the third time,
a gunman opens fire a few
miles from my home.

This year, another young woman
turns up dead, another brown boy
murdered for holding anything in his hands.

Another siren closing down the schools,
grocery stores, post office, movie theatres.

This year, the last white male rhino died,
pushing the species into extinction.

SCULLERY

This morning, the news suggests
we stay inside. Another person building out
their empire of incidents.

But the highway stays slogged,
the supermarket bloated with shoppers
as I pick through peaches.

I think that perhaps Sarah's house too
is an exercise in continuing.

TOILETTE

I've taken up running for reasons
I won't read into. A group of young girls
hush to one another in the gym. Congregations
of lean legs. Smell of soap you know
came in the shape of daisies.
Froth on the girls' mouths, each salivating over
the other one's Me Too moment. Testing
with scrutiny to see who smiled through
it the hardest. Who forgot it happened the fastest.
Meanwhile, outside, the men in workpants pull
at the statues on the university's lawns—Lilliputians
bringing down expired giants with rope
and sets of pins. The girls, even in their School
of Grief, recognize the thud.

SITTING ROOM

When you are a
beautiful woman you have

certain responsibilities.
When you are a smart woman
no one expects a thing.

But appetites, like solar systems,
are ever expanding.

Time crushes
us like a pill
under a paperweight.

Here in the heat
of the South crickets groan
in constant congress.

The weather beckons love
one moment, flood the next.

Another puddle
of stallions. Another Ophelia
in the river. Silent
reminders

of grace on its way
to the grave.

CUPOLA

By the fifth renovation,
Sarah had become somewhat
of an oddity.

Would take tea only with her sister
who would wonder aloud
if Sarah had resigned herself
to living alone forever.

Sarah and her sister did not see
the same ghosts.

But if you do catch sight of a woman
trapped in a tower, know that it is okay
to assume she is cursed.

Just do not assume
that she is not looking down
from said tower at you
in your very small armor

thinking the very same thing.

THE ARMORY

To the lovers of my life,
I am sorry for pulling away first.

The instinct goes back
generations.

When my Mamita would call the
the office, he was always

out to lunch,

but when he'd come home
he'd be starving.

Maybe that is why
she took up cigarettes,
even though

she always said she was
too small for smoking.
Maybe that is why
she warns me about becoming
a suspicious woman,

says that there are certain
things better left
unearthed.

She doesn't know that my lover
holds me like a loaded gun,
afraid of the way

I fire.

ATTIC

The formidable years are only now upon me,
and what a luxury it's been to believe
in my own visions, to have had faith this far.

But I regret to say the mystery of this life
has not yet opened its coat to me, has not revealed
the shiny pocket watches and baubles therein.

I don't want to be scared of what I can't see
but the future has its back turned to me.

MUSIC ROOM

If architecture is, as Goethe says
frozen music, then maybe my poems
are each a fixed point and not at all
the cannibalized piano sounds I perceive
them to be.

And Sarah's house, not just a house,
but rather her illegible self
demanding to be pressed into a shape
it cannot possibly hold.

DOOR

The years pass and
rooms go on being built,
doors continue
their disjointed dance.

Sarah dies in The Daisy Room.
It's 1923. The house lets in
its first guest.

DOOR

The story perpetuates itself.
A nation pins its unease
on one woman.

A year ago, a final room
found behind slats of wood.

The Universe's grand gesture.

Just when you thought you
were approaching the close,
a wall reveals itself.

What we build
we build forever.

GARDEN

We end at the heart
of life's cipher.

Flora and fauna
in Fibonacci sequence,

daisies, lilies, buck-
wheat and rye.

Sarah, you saw the inside
from the inside.

A cocoon cracks open.
A mother delivers a worm.

To make it this far
and not leave behind the details.

When I get to the center
I will not leave behind the details.

These souls must be simultaneous
with the ochre sky.

Phantasmagoria at the Garden Party

It was another day spent looking
at the weather and thinking about myself.

I could not see the sun inside the wood
but I was sure of it anyway.

Just like the quality of a poet,
to see a storm and believe it's theirs.

The grand secret we toss into at night
always quiet and supine beside us—

that anything can be magic
if it catches you off guard.

You must let enough of the day rush at you
unprepared for even the smallest

coin, green moss on the underside
of a gray stone, dead bird by the feeder.

On and on the light inside
the skull will spin and you will take

rides from strangers,
refusing to see what's coming

because who walks away
from magic? Cruel or otherwise.

The woman you drove by,
clipping flowers in the empty field.

Rain that was in no one's way
today. The surprise you felt

when your dog brought you back
his plush chew toy torn open

and inside a bright red heart.

Liminal Residency

She says she wants to get right up
to the edge.
I mean to ask her of what
but it slips my mind.
Instead we watch
the silver moon dissolve
over the cedars,
a hundred marzipan birds
twisting in warped delight.
We watch from the windowsill,
a sort-of edge, an easy one granted.
Although there are always
characters in books who never
even make it that far.
The living room TV is alight
with the name
of another missing woman.
Last seen in Beaumont buying a box
of tampons and some spearmint.
The awful thoughts sit like marbles
in their silken pouch,
waiting for me to palm one
into the room, out of
its colossal darkness.
The evening gnats
circling the head like
a halo on a garbage angel.
But the wind, it looked clean
pushing its way past the ferns.
And the vanilla blooms were bulbing
in the swamps, sending
their scent to us in the night,
pressing against
the smell of warm trash
and sweaty kelp, so that in that moment
despite it all, we felt clean too.

These Days

Have I missed all the moments where you held fruit
to the light, turning the melon slices into jewels?

Did I miss the part where you frayed slightly, then unraveled
all at once? How beautiful you must've been in that heap.

And I flew right through it all didn't I? Flew past you
confessing your secrets before taking the shot.

Like we were cheersing the day in elementary school you put
another boy's penis in your mouth because you were

both curious and nothing more. Had I stopped to play it out
maybe I'd have seen simply how you could become a man

of integrity. How you would reveal to me all the ways in which
my life was not useless. Now in the low light of the living room

you tell me of the teens these days who don't believe Helen Keller
was a real person, and I sit wishing it was 100 years ago,

but without any of the bad parts. Does disbelieving the existence
of a person make that person disappear? I disbelieve my own

existence all the time. When people treat pennies like luck.
When the gooseneck kettle spits out boiling water without ever

offering a whistle for warning. I didn't feel real the day I quit ballet
because the thought of moving my body through space

seemed impossible. Even then, at six, I knew what it meant
to be alive but to misunderstand so many seconds of it.

I question your existence, too, and that is when I am truly
the worst. But I do it over and over, taking you mostly

for granted, because the moment I remember I have not
imagined you is the moment the world returns to focus.

Two of Cups

Back when the earth had two twin moons
weren't we those moons?
Birds with their necks in crescendo,
bright backsides fanned out in full.
In the field with the lions,
their mouths open for a feeding
it was you who said there was no monster
you wouldn't love for me.
Every lifetime the crowds
give us new names, by now
we should have thousands. Each iteration
bluer than the last.
We could destroy each other
with these many eyes.
Crack the champagne flute
in half, turn the sharp part outward.
But even at the left turns of life
when you are spending
all of your time
imagining we are fucking,
I will spend all my time imagining
we are two people in a painting,
fucking. And each time we will come out
so beautiful, as if we are saying goodbye.

Unmoved Mover

Brian's father just spent his seventieth birthday in Antarctica,
eating sticks of butter to stave off the cold. At least, that's how
I imagine him, in his navy parka, boots scattering beams of light.
When I see him next I know it will be hard to avoid
the question of melting but I am certain that he brought along
a good book and it will be easy to make a swift subject change.
I know this isn't the only way to keep going, but I am not majestic
like the rat, able to chew through what keeps it from being free.
When I became a poet I was told by other poets that my job
would be mostly lighting the inside of birdhouses
or shoveling snow off the stubborn hydrangeas.
To be always a ceaseless machine of spitting wonder.
But even now I know I am not in love with the apples
the way a poet should be. Never managed to open the door
on all that fine art. If I have gotten good at anything,
it is at blindly running into rooms
only to find my lover in bed with someone who has my face
but isn't me. Do I believe them when they say they didn't know?
Of course I do, and slowly I slide in between them
letting what comes next last.

This Is The Job

Turning everyone into rivers
or delicate dodos, built to go extinct. Falling
into the habit of turning people out of body entirely,
seeing only the substitute shapes.

The dark outline of an art thief meticulously unstitching
the canvas. A pair of crossed fingers tattooed
on the lower back of a lover.

Brianna explains the shelf life of blood, 34 days if refrigerated,
and I am caught helpless at how she moves
the science with her hair. Even the buildings now,
absolved of absoluteness, seem nothing more than metal
stripped clean, which is spark.

It would all be frightening if it weren't somehow easier.
The world coming inch by inch into focus.
And from far away what was a fire is actually the perfect geometry
of a honeycomb cluster, the waffling of a tree plunged
with peach and citrus. What was a smile in the crowd

turns to an early-in-the-month moon. The metaphor
always earns more of the mystery anyway.
Like the first time you walked into

the room and not a single head turned. How that was the best of it.
Floating above the magic show, staring at a woman sparkling
under such large axes. A breath-held audience to leave guessing.
The proscenium a vision of velvet and rabbit.

Rabies

Summer fought back hard this year.
I swore I saw a man blurry
in the underbrush, looking through a scope
he'd fashioned with his fingers.
In the opiated afternoon, the lovers
fuck unencumbered. Standing fan
on high, too hot to walk the dog.
The old woman's home shows signs
of a mind slipping into water.
Ants in the sugarbowl, smell of burnt
sourdough stretching in an oven.
He tells me to be honest
because not saying anything
would be worse than a flat out lie.
Outside a large bugzapper comes to light
after conjoining with the small body
of an arthropod. Soundtrack to the many
awful dreams had as a child.
In truth, I am over this abundance
of mirrors. Of always arriving late
to the reading of the will.
The dog that bit my mother the summer
she was twelve was posturing
for a rub on its underside. Invited her in
then unprovoked it attacked.
In the middle of a heat wave,
one might think there is no such thing
as reprieve, but the shells of slain creatures
litter the asphalt. Excessive sun having
broken their bodies in twain, so
something remaining might escape.
What would crack out of me
would most likely never return.
The schoolyard across
the street has just let out,
the sweaty boys returning
to their basements to smoke weed.
One boy sits on the curb, catching
my eye when I walk out for the mail.

I could offer him a glass of water
while he waits, but I don't.
It's not that he frightens me,
he just reminds me of the dog
that bit my mother. Heart slender
as a silverfish, teeth glistening
in the blurred waves of afternoon.
The doctor had to slide
fourteen needles into my mother's belly.
All because she loved a thing
that was scared of being loved.

Busby Berkeley Girl

There was a time when I was unaware of my own blush.
A time when there were still pieces of men I couldn't name.
But what was once easy is now hurling myself through
Mondays and missed phone calls, preconceived plans
I'm welcome to join in on,—or become a pile of leaves.
Become the kind of person who must think up
different ways to approach people. The kind of woman
who sees patterns in rows of parked cars, in the thick slabs
of meat hanging from butchers' windows, all the while wondering
If I acknowledge   that I think I am more
          important than I really am   have I just created a paradox?
There is a word for this dense meanwhile of being.
There is a word for when one confuses themself for a Thing.
Deep down I know I am not a Thing because I do not possess
the quality of objects, resolute in the way they take up space.
I am refractions of light against mirrors—the out of focus vampire
in the family photo, who knows very little of being carved from stone.

New Sincerity

/

Today the rain is only a mile away
and it will keep coming
says the weatherman.
I read in a biology book that trees
have linked root systems
so they may share essential nutrients.
This is very socialist of the trees
so of course people are suspicious.
If it keeps raining they will
have no choice
but to pass back and forth
so much water they will
eventually drown and this
is the best metaphor
I can think of for love.
The famous poet says I cannot fit
the entire world into a poem
no matter how many *Things*
I find homes for.
But the famous poet does not know
how small the world really is
compared to this poem. And really
it's okay. I didn't believe either
but one day a woman lassoed
a strand of her hair
around the body of a fly
and walked it in mid-air
like a dog on a leash.

//

Poetry, I was your daughter.
Poetry, I was your gilded cow.
Look at how the maidens
tied flowers to my mane
then walked me miles in the desert
to swallow your dogma. Poetry,
I was hit in the head as a child
and things only got better
from there. Poetry, I've never
known what needs
explaining first,
the arrow or the bow
the seamstress or the king. Poetry,
for years I've been faithful
and patient in this silo
dreaming and thinking
about those dreams.
Not necessarily what happens in them
—the cactus, the hairpin
fracture, the factory for making
baby dolls, with the chutes
of tiny hands and toes,
heads kept precious
in the back.
No, I have been thinking
about where you go Poetry
when I am in those dreams,
for in them we are
never together.
I don't think about you once,
how sad.

///

I never agreed to this.
Someone writes a book
about a woman burning and now
that woman burns forever.
In the aged paperback

about summer in Algiers
a young man traps a mouse inside
some prose without an offering
of cheese or a wheel for frivolity
and honestly the whole gig
has gotten tiring if you ask me.
There are other ways
to be an *artist*
my artist friend tells me as she 3-D
prints another dick, this time
pink with glitter. Soon she will
have enough dicks to fill
an entire gallery.
How I wish I could cut through
light like her.

          ////

For so long I thought
I was good, and then
for so long I fought
to actually be good,
and still nothing.
Still I am a selfish hub of stars,
the antipode of
wherever I am supposed to be.
The famous poet
tells us that poetry
is a room with
only windows.
The famous poet
does not believe
in doors.
I didn't
        believe either,
        but the barker
        at the carnival still takes
        time every night
        to empty plastic bags
        of un-won goldfish
        back into the creek.

Meanwhile,
deep underground
the unpronounceable
name of G-d waits
to make an entrance.

All Good Things Must Come to an Erratum

Of course there'd be mistakes.
Fist fights at the silent disco,
every *I love you too, but*—
and how quickly I forgot
the correct way to play chess.
There were police sirens
in Georgia, shining up the night
the way pet scans light bodies
carrying tumors into Christmas.
There were men who never made it
to my bed and briars stuck to
shoe soles from walking through
the roses. I won't lie to you.
It has taken too long to learn
how little it hurts
being happy for other people.
And then there is the matter
of a stolen silver book pin
with his grandmother's
name engraved. I hope
he's not still looking.
To be alive and to wish
otherwise. To consider myself
a creature of empathy, only
to eat all of the meat.
Suppose a moment
that something can be
both beautiful and cliché.
The bird bouncing off
the windshield, the smell
of smoke when there are no fires.
The deer outside the barn
who stay so still they must be
listening. I'm sorry
for not knowing that beauty,
even the reoccurring kind,
is enough to be thankful for.
And while it took time,
the animals have forgiven me

my behemoth appetites.
My mother has forgiven me
for my junkyard years, the rust
I let settle on the spoons.
And all of my future mistakes:
the canned goods wasted,
the tower of half made plans,
continuing to choose
poetry, even when poetry
refuses to choose me back.
I do not yet know who
will forgive me for these.
But I do know that while I regret
two out of three
of the piercings, I do not regret
any of my bloody hands.
The night spent stranded
on the roof
while the ladder lay
flat in the grass.
How liberating it was
owning up to where
it all went wrong.

Doorknob Comments

Here I go again, confusing confession
for a finale, hand on the doorknob
of the therapist's office, when finally I find it in me to
share the juicy bits, to talk about
the tendrils of peas Mother shuffled

in the colander, the low-slung greenery
suffocating the infants, their small hands slapping
to Miss Mary Mack and all those silver buttons.
You asked if it got overwhelming?

Yes, all overwhelming, like walking past
a Salvation Army Santa. Like water coming
up from the cracks in the bathroom tile, right when
you must go so badly. All that water hinting

at the lake lying beneath the bathroom.
The bodies dumped, the trash fish wrapped
in six-pack plastic. Bottle opener, small tin filled
with baby teeth, the mucky baubles
of lost love. There you are, just trying to pee,
but not without the whole universe

interrupting. It reminds me of the one
about the brother and sister who had to split up
all of their parents' belongings: the davenport desk,
ceramic kettles, handmade quilts,
and Christmas ornaments. Everything going

according to plan until they unearthed a small
hole in the inseam of their father's work suit,
and hidden therein, a marble that looked like Earth.
Both children wanted the marble badly,
neither spoke to the other ever again.

Love isn't the same as happiness. Some poet
probably said that. And maybe what we yearn
for is really just the jack-o'-lantern in the room
offering light through its ghoulish grin.

By now it should be clear that these dreams of ours
are brutes. Alluding to a life beyond commercials
at the cliffhangers, beyond the strangers waiting
in the next room for their turn to recall trauma.

My mother recently went with her friend Lynne
to a metempsychosis meeting.
Found out they've been related in more than one
past life, and that made me sad or jealous
but mostly relieved because it meant

that maybe in another life I had been her mother,
and the only thing certain about death
is that we must take turns.

Suddenly the rest seemed silly.
Demanding love from even a mother;
expecting that poetry, of all things, ought to tell the truth.

Today, the sun was strong. Earth felt like
a pristine blue egg, and for the first time in months
I didn't consider any of it to be for me.

Notes

The title and first line of "The Breakup of My Country" are inspired by James Tate's "The Nitrogen Cycle."

The poem, "When I Was Sixteen" is inspired by Laura Kasischke's poem "Babysitter."

The poem "A Busby Berkley Girl" quotes a line from Ian Bogost's "Alien Phenomenology, or What It's Like to Be a Thing."

The title of "The Dead and I Sing Behind the Rhododendron Bushes" is taken from a line in Virginia Woolf's *Mrs. Dalloway*.

The poem "What We Build" was heavily inspired by the story of Sarah Winchester and her San Jose mansion. Thank you to the following texts and authors that helped shape that piece. Richard Allen Wagner for his "Truth About Sarah Winchester" and to Mary Jo Ignoffo, author of *Captive of the Labyrinth*.

Acknowledgments

Earlier versions of these poems have been featured in the following publications and anthologies: *Narrative Magazine, Colorado Review, Zone 3 Press, Sonora Review, New Ohio Review, Meridian, Frontier Poetry, The Indiana Review, Four Way Review, Carve Magazine, Sugar House Review, the minnesota review, Radar Poetry, Prime Number Magazine, The Southampton Review.* Thanks to the editors and journals who first published these poems.

To the writers and mentors who helped this book become a real object, I owe you a debt of gratitude. To Tayve, Matt, Halee, and the rest of the Trio House team, for not only choosing the book, but for helping me turn it into something truly special, thank you for your *Yes.* Thank you, to the New Writers Project at UT and the amazing professors and cohort who saw early versions of these poems and inspired many more that came after. To Carrie Fountain, thank you for your unparalleled guidance and support at every step of this journey. And to Bethany Hegedus for giving me a home away from home with the Writing Barn.

Mom and Dad, the poems are for you, because of you.

Brian, thank you for our beautiful life and the supreme love you instilled in me.

And to the rest of my friends and family, whose care and belief in this book, and in me, never waivered, I am overwhelmed with love and appreciation. You are what makes this world such a wild and wonderful thing to write about.

About the Author

Jessica Hincapie grew up in South Florida, nestled between the Everglades' swamps and the sandy coasts of the Atlantic. She holds an MFA in Poetry from the University of Texas where she received the Michael Adams Prize in Poetry. Her other honors include a Pushcart Prize nomination, finalist for Radar's Coniston Prize, a Cuttyhunk Writers Residency, and she was recently featured in *Narrative Magazine's 30 Below* (30 Emerging Writers under 30). She has poems out in *Colorado Review, Gulf Coast, Indiana Review, New Ohio Review, The Southampton Review, Meridian* and elsewhere. Currently she is the Program Director of the Writing Barn, a writing workshop and retreat space in South Austin. She teaches Creative Writing to kids and adults across the country.

About the Artist

Tori Baisden is a Creative Director, Designer, and Partner at Utendahl Creative. She came of age in the swamps of South Florida where she developed an enduring love for make-believe. That passion led her to New York where she helps lead Utendahl Creative as the studio's Creative Director. She's worked on projects for Target, GoPuff, LaDiDa, HumanCo, Good Thing Going, Rooftop Films, and many more. Her work has been featured in Forbes and the Dieline, recognized by the Webby Awards and Hermes Creative Awards, and she has participated as a judge for the D&AD Young Blood awards. Her creative practice is fueled by empathy, storytelling, long breaks, and a desire to stir up trouble.

About the Book

Bloomer was designed at Trio House Press through the collaboration of:

Matt Mauch, Lead Editor
Halee Kirkwood, Supporting Editor
Hadley Hendrix, Assistant Editor
Tori Baisden, Cover Design
Matt Mauch, Interior Design

The text is set in Adobe Caslon Pro.

The publication of this book is made possible, whole or in part,
by the generous support of the following individuals or agencies:

Anonymous

About the Press

Trio House Press is an independent literary press publishing three or more collections of poems annually. Our Mission is to promote poetry as a literary art enhancing culture and the human experience. We offer two annual poetry awards: the Trio Award for First or Second Book for emerging poets and the Louise Bogan Award for Artistic Merit and Excellence for a book of poems contributing in an innovative and distinct way to poetry. We also offer an annual open reading period for manuscript publication.

Trio House Press adheres to and supports all ethical standards and guidelines outlined by the CLMP.

Trio House Press, Inc. is dedicated to the promotion of poetry as literary art, which enhances the human experience and its culture. We contribute in an innovative and distinct way to poetry by publishing emerging and established poets, providing educational materials, and fostering the artistic process of writing poetry. For further information, or to consider making a donation to Trio House Press, please visit us online at www.triohousepress.org.

Other Trio House Press books you might enjoy:

Unceded Land by Issam Zineh / 2022

The Fallow by Megan Neville / 2021 Trio Award Winner selected by Steve Healey

The Traditional Feel of the Ballroom by Hannah Gamble / 2021

Third Winter in Our Second Country by Andres Rojas / 2021

Sweet Beast by Gabriella R. Tallmadge / 2020 Louise Bogan Award Winner selected by Sandy Longhorn

Songbox by Kirk Wilson / 2020 Trio Award Winner selected by Malena Mörling

YOU DO NOT HAVE TO BE GOOD by Madeleine Barnes / 2020

X-Rays and Other Landscapes by Kyle McCord / 2019

Threed, This Road Not Damascus by Tamara J. Madison / 2019

My Afmerica by Artress Bethany White / 2018 Trio Award Winner selected by Sun Yung Shin

Waiting for the Wreck to Burn by Michele Battiste / 2018 Louise Bogan Award Winner selected by Jeff Friedman

Cleave by Pamel Johnson Parker / 2018 Trio Award Winner selected by Jennifer Barber

Two Towns Over by Darren C. Demaree / 2018 Louise Bogan Award Winner selected by Campbell McGrath

Bird~Brain by Matt Mauch / 2017

Dark Tussock Moth by Mary Cisper / 2016 Trio Award Winner selcted by Bhisham Bherwani

The Short Drive Home by Joe Osterhaus / 2016 Louise Bogan Award Winner selected by Chard DeNiord

Break the Habit by Tara Betts / 2016

Bone Music by Stephen Cramer / 2015 Louise Bogan Award Winner selected by Kimiko Hahn

Rigging a Chevy into a Time Machine and Other Ways to Escape a Plague by Carolyn Hembree / 2015 Trio Award Winner selected by Neil Shepard

Magpies in the Valley of Oleanders by Kyle McCord / 2015

Your Immaculate Heart by Annmarie O'Connell / 2015

The Alchemy of My Mortal Form by Sandy Longhorn / 2014 Louise Bogan Award Winner selected by Peter Campion

What the Night Numbered by Bradford Tice / 2014 Trio Award Winner selected by Carol Frost

Flight of August by Lawrence Eby / 2013 Louise Bogan Award Winner selected by Joan Houlihan

The Consolations by John W. Evans / 2013 Trio Award Winner selected by Mihaela Moscaliuc

Fellow Odd Fellow by Stephen Riel / 2013

Clay by David Groff / 2012 Louise Bogan Award Winner selected by Michael Waters

Gold Passage by Iris Jamahl Dunkle / 2012 Trio Award Winner selected by Ross Gay

If You're Lucky Is a Theory of Mine by Matt Mauch / 2012

CPSIA information can be obtained
at www.ICGtesting.com
Printed in the USA
BVHW051448210622
640292BV00006B/713